WHEELS AND CRANKS

ANGELA ROYSTON

Heinemann Library
Chicago, Illinois

Customer Service 888-454-2279
Visit our website at www.heinemannlibrary.com

Designed by Visual Image
Illustrations by Barry Atkinson
Originated by Dot Gradations
Printed in China

05
10 9 8 7 6 5 4

Library of Congress Cataloging-in-Publication Data
Royston. Angela.
    Wheels and cranks / Angela Royston.
        p. cm. – (Machines in action)
    Includes bibliographical references and index.
    ISBN 1-57572-324-7 (HC), 1-4034-4089-1 (Pbk.)
    1. Wheels—Juvenile literature. 2. Cranks and crankshafts—Juvenile literature.
    [1. Wheels. 2. Cranks and crankshafts.] I. Title. II. Series.

TJ181.5. .R69 2000
621.8'11—dc21
                                          00-035024

Acknowledgments
The author and publishers are grateful to the following for permission to reproduce copyright material: Cephas / Nigel Blythe, p. 19; Cumulus / Trevor Clifford, pp. 17, 22; Ecoscene / Sally Morgan, p. 23; Heinemann/ Trevor Clifford, pp. 9, 24, 28, 29; Still Pictures / Jorgen Schytte, p. 18; Pictor Uniphoto, pp. 8, 11, 26; Popperfoto / Pierre Boussel, p. 4; Robert Harding Picture Library / p. 5; The Stock Market / Lester Lefkowitz p. 13; Telegraph Colour Library / D. Redfern p. 25; Tony Stone Images / Mark Wagner, p. 7, Tony Stone Images / Aldo Torelli, p. 10, Tony Stone Images / Andy Sacks, p. 12; Courtesy of the Trustees of the Victoria and Albert Museum, p. 15

Cover photograph reproduced with permission of Science Photo Library.

Every effort has been made to contact copyright holders of any material reproduced in this book. Any omissions will be rectified in subsequent printings if notice is given to the publisher.

Some words are shown in bold, **like this.** You can find out what they mean by looking in the glossary.

CONTENTS

What Do Wheels Do?

Most vehicles that move on land use wheels to help them move fast and easily.

How can you move faster than you can run? The answer is by using a machine, such as a car, train, or other form of transportation. Most vehicles use an **engine** to give them power, but you do not need an engine to move faster. A set of wheels is all you need. Using a bicycle or skateboard, you will soon overtake all but the fastest runners.

Think about it!

No one knows who invented the wheel, but it was used about 5,500 years ago to make clay pots. The wheel was connected to a foot pedal by a crank. As the wheel turned, the pot spun around fast and evenly.

Wheels and cranks

Wheels also make it easier to carry things. Vans, trucks, cars, and baby buggies are all designed to carry goods or people. If you put a handle on one side of a wheel you can use the handle to turn the wheel. The handle is called a **crank**.

A wheel is a simple machine. It is so simple that you might not think of it as a machine at all. This book looks at how wheels work and at some of the many ways that wheels and cranks make our lives easier.

Rollers

The Ancient Egyptians built huge pyramids with very large blocks of stone. They probably used tree trunks as rollers to help them drag the blocks across the ground.

Before wheels were invented, people probably used **rollers** to help them move heavy loads. And the first rollers would have been tree trunks. The Ancient Egyptians probably used rollers thousands of years ago to help them build the pyramids. Each block of stone was dragged over the rollers by gangs of workers.

Although rollers help to move something forward or backward, the rollers themselves stay in the same place. As each roller turns around it moves the load a little bit farther.

Rollers in industry

Many factories use rollers to move heavy things along. Sometimes a **conveyor belt** is stretched over two or more turning rollers. The end roller is turned around by an **engine** and it moves the belt around.

These rollers help to load cargo onto the plane.

Try this!

Make a set of rollers with about eight round pencils. Place the pencils side by side with a space between them. Place a pile of books on top of the pencils and push it forward. Move the back pencil to the front as it becomes clear.

Spokes and Tires

The first wheels were probably solid wood—a slice of a thick tree trunk rubbed round and smooth. Such wheels would have been very heavy. As **carpenters** became more skillful, they cut out parts of the wheel between the **rim** and the **hub** in the middle. This left thin **spokes** that joined the hub to the rim. Wheels with spokes were still very strong, but were much lighter than solid wheels.

The wheels on this carriage are made of wood. A metal hoop has been attached to the outside of the rim to keep the wood from wearing away.

Make it work!

Design a model car or buggy using empty boxes, jars, and junk. What do you think will make the best wheels—bottle tops, balls, thread spools, or jar lids? Try rolling different things down a slope to see which is the best.

Rubber tires are filled with air, like a thick balloon. When the wheel hits a bump it is squeezed and then bounces back into shape. The people inside the car hardly feel the bump at all.

Tires

Wooden wheels bump and jump over every hole and stone in the road. When motor cars were invented just over a hundred years ago, a new wheel was invented too. It was covered with a rubber tire which was filled with air. Today's tires are still filled with air. They are made of rubber mixed with steel to make them stronger and help them last longer.

Bicycle wheels are also covered with a thick rubber tire. Inside is a thinner rubber tire that is pumped full of air.

Friction

A racing car speeds around the track on wide, smooth tires. Each tire costs a lot of money and soon wears out.

If you roll a model car along the floor, it moves fast at first but soon slows down and stops. It slows down because the wheels stick slightly on the floor. The sticking is called **friction**.

Smooth wheels stick less than rough wheels. Racing cars have smooth wide wheels. They are wide so they are less likely to skid sideways. Trains have smooth narrow wheels. The wheels run on tracks so they cannot skid sideways at all.

The wheels inside some machines are covered in a thin layer of oil to make them run more smoothly.

10

Why wheels work

Why is it easier to push a shopping cart of food than to push a box of the same weight across the floor? If a wheel is free to roll, it moves forward as it turns. There is little friction at the **hub** of the wheel to stop it from turning. Only a small area of each wheel touches the floor at any time, so there is less friction between the wheels and the ground than between a heavy box and the ground.

The train's smooth, metal wheels move along the shiny track. There is little friction to slow the wheels down.

Try this!

Use a model car to test different surfaces. Make a slope by leaning a plank of wood against a box. Now put the model car at the top of the slope and let it run down. Measure how far it runs across the floor before it stops. Repeat the experiment on different kinds of floor. Try a wooden floor, carpet, and tile. Which floor has the least friction?

Treads

If there was no **friction** between a wheel and the ground, the wheel would just spin around without moving forward. Rubber tires grip the ground and help to push the wheel forward.

This tractor has big wheels and tires. The tires have very deep treads to keep from slipping on muddy ground.

Some tires have deep grooves cut into them to give more grip. The grooves are called **treads**. Treads help the driver control the car or truck. Wet or icy roads are much more slippery than dry roads. As the wheel turns, the tread pushes water away so the tire runs over drier road.

Think about it!

Why do racing bikes have large wheels with thin, smooth tires, while mountain bikes have smaller wheels with thick tires and deep treads?

Big wheels

Some vehicles are driven over rough ground where there is no road at all. Tractors can drive through muddy fields where cars or trucks would get stuck in the mud. When a car wheel gets stuck in wet mud, it spins around but cannot grip the ground to move forward. Big wheels with deep treads bite into the mud.

The wheels of this dump truck are bigger than the driver! The dump truck carries heavy loads over rough, loose ground.

13

Cam Wheels

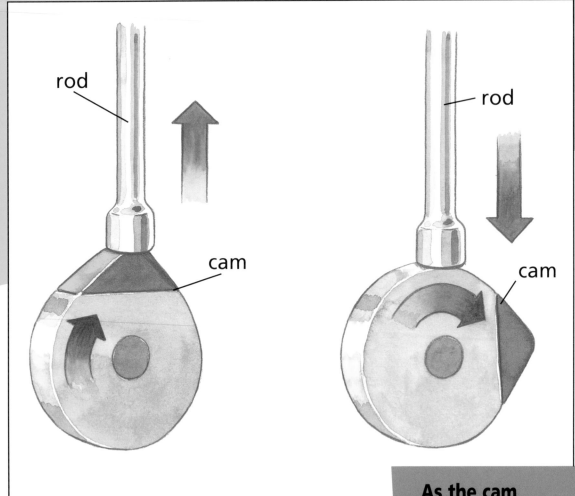

rod

cam

rod

cam

A **cam wheel** is a wheel which is not completely circular. Part of the **rim** sticks out, like a knob, from the rest of the rim. A cam is used to move a rod up and down or in and out. The rod touches the rim of the wheel. As the wheel turns, the knob pushes the rod up. The rod then moves back into place until the knob pushes it up again.

As the cam wheel turns around, the red block lifts the hammer up. As the block moves past, the hammer falls again.

Uses of cams

Cams can be many different shapes. Some cams have several knobs, while others are oval-shaped. Each cam is shaped to do a particular job.

Many toys have parts that move up and down, to beat drums, for example. They probably have cams inside them. If you have any toys like these that are old and broken, try to open them up to look inside. Have an adult help you, and be careful—there may be sharp pieces inside.

Make it work!

Do a drawing for a fairground ride that uses a cam to move a horse or boat up and down.

A cam inside this model raises the drummer's arms.

What Do Cranks Do?

A **crank** handle is an easy way to make a wheel turn. It is fixed to the **hub** of the wheel. The **pedals** on an old-fashioned bicycle are crank handles. As the **cyclist** turns the pedals in a small circle, the **rim** of the wheel moves around in a big circle. As the cyclist turns the pedals slowly, the rim moves fast to keep up.

This bicycle was popular over 100 years ago. The cyclist turned the pedals at the hub of the front wheel to move the bicycle forward.

Large crank handles

The handle of the pencil sharpener is joined to a metal rod. It is still a crank handle because it makes the rod turn. The handle of the pencil sharpener turns in a big circle while the rod turns in a small circle. The small force needed to turn the handle becomes a big force that is used to sharpen the pencil.

The handle on this pencil sharpener turns the sharpener. Instead of holding the sharpener and turning the pencil, the blade turns and the pencil stays still.

Think about it!

Find out which of these use a crank handle to make them work— a hand-operated sewing machine, a car window handle, or a fishing reel.

Cranks in Action

The oxen are turning a wooden **crank** handle. The wooden handle is joined to an **axle** or rod. As the axle turns, it turns the machinery that pumps the water. The oxen need to use only a small amount of **effort** at the end of the handle to produce a strong **force** at the center.

As the oxen walk slowly around in a circle, the wooden handles turn to help pump out water.

An axle is a rod or bar that joins two wheels. Sometimes the axle moves around with the wheels. Sometimes the axle stays still and the wheels turn on it.

Try this!

You will need two pieces of strong wire. Make a U-shape in the middle of one piece of wire. Hook the other piece of wire over the U-shape to make a crank. As you twist the first piece of wire, the crank should move back and forth.

thread spools

The woman turns her spinning wheel by pushing the pedal up and down with her foot. The wheel spins very fast.

The spinning wheel

A crank handle in the spinning wheel changes the up-and-down movement of the pedal into a circular movement. It can do this because it has a bend in it. Can you see how the crank goes around when the **pedal** moves up and down?

A Pedal Car

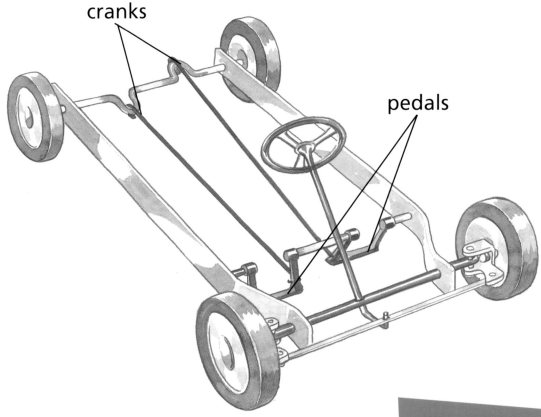

cranks

pedals

A **pedal** car uses **cranks** and an **axle** to turn the wheels. When you push the red pedal forward, the red crank pulls the back axle around until the red loop is facing forward. Which way is the blue loop in the axle now facing? Pushing the blue pedal forward makes the blue crank pull the back axle around further. So pushing one pedal then the other turns the back axle of the car. The wheels are joined to the axle and turn with it.

The pedals in the pedal car turn the axle to make the back wheels spin. The steering wheel is joined to a rod which moves another axle to turn the front wheels right or left.

Make it work!

Design a fan that uses a foot pedal and a crank to make it work. Think about the blades of the fan. What shape should they be to move the air?

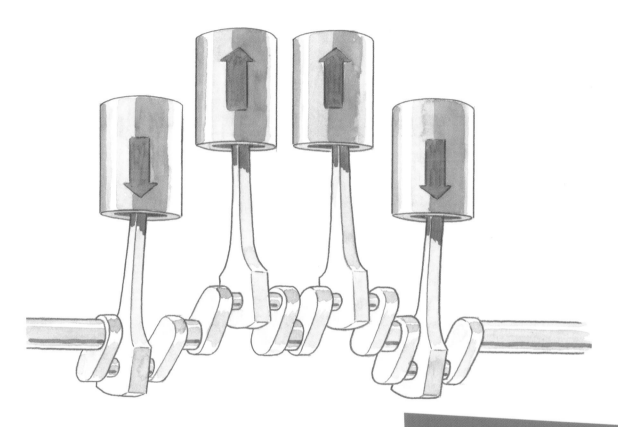

Steering

The steering wheel is joined to the steering rod. The small force needed to turn the steering wheel turns the steering rod with a strong force. The steering rod has a bend at the bottom. When the bend moves to the left or the right, it pulls the front axle to turn the wheels.

The four pistons in a gasoline engine go up and down. Can you see how the pistons turn the drive shaft? The drive shaft is connected by other axles to the wheels.

Using the Wind to Turn Wheels

When the wind blows, it catches the sails of the toy windmill and pushes them around. The sails turn the metal rod. As it turns it looks as if the man is turning the **crank** handle. The turning rod winds up the string that is joined to a bucket in the well. When the wind stops blowing, the weight of the bucket unwinds the string.

When the wind turns the sails, the crank handle turns and winds up the bucket in the well.

Wind turbine

The long blades of the **turbine** catch the wind and spin around. The turbine uses the spinning to make electricity. The whole turbine can turn on the pole so that the blades always face the wind.

The blades of the turbine are very long. Some wind turbines have blades which are as long as half a soccer field. They are mounted on very high poles!

The wind turns the blades of the wind turbine. As the blades turn they drive a generator inside the box behind them. The generator makes electricity.

Think about it!

In the past, windmills were used to turn grind stones to grind corn. They had huge sails instead of the long, thin sails of modern wind turbines. Do you think it took more wind or less wind to turn the windmill's sails than it takes to turn the wind turbine's blades?

Water Wheels

The weight of the falling water pushes the water wheel around.

When you pour water onto the water wheel, the weight of the water pushes the blade down. This turns the wheel and brings another blade under the falling water. The weight of the falling water pushes this blade down and so the wheel keeps turning.

Make it work!

Use a jug of water and a water-wheel toy to find out what makes the wheel turn fastest. Try pouring a little water and then a lot. Pour the water from just above the wheel and then pour it from high above the wheel. What is the best way to keep the wheel turning fast?

The ship's engine turns the paddle wheel to pull the boat through the water.

Paddle wheels

Two hundred years ago, the first big cotton mills were built next to rivers. The flowing river turned a big water wheel which turned an **axle**. The axle was connected to the machines in the factory. In the summer, the rivers had less water in them. What effect do you think this had on the machines?

Falling water makes a wheel turn. Similarly, a turning paddle wheel pulls the water through it. As the water is pulled back, the boat is pushed forward.

Water Power

A deep lake of water is held in by the dam built across the valley. The lake is filled by streams or rivers flowing into it.

A **hydroelectric power station** uses the force of moving water to make electricity. A large pipe near the bottom of the dam wall allows a stream of water to leave the lake. The stream flows through the blades of the **turbine**. The turning blades are joined to a **shaft** and to machinery that makes electricity. The electricity is taken to homes and factories along thick electric wires.

Make it work!

Find out why the turbine in a hydroelectric power station takes water from the bottom of the lake. Use three identical plastic bottles. Ask an adult to make a hole with a corkscrew near the top of the first bottle, in the middle of the second bottle, and near the bottom of the third bottle. Fill each bottle with water. Which bottle gives the most powerful spurt of water?

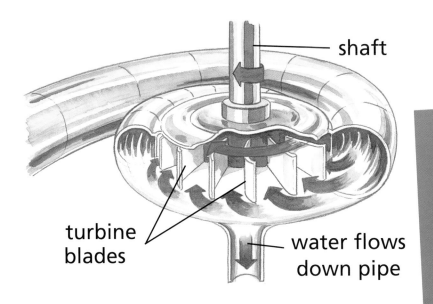

shaft

turbine blades

water flows down pipe

As the water flows between the blades, it turns the wheel. The wheel turns the shaft. The turning shaft is used to make electricity.

Controlling the flow

Homes, offices, and factories use less electricity at night. In a hydroelectric power station it is easy to control how much electricity is made. When a gate at the entrance to the pipe, deep in the lake, is closed, no water escapes and so no electricity is made. When the gate is partly closed, less water flows into the pipe, so the shaft spins more slowly and makes less electricity.

Make a Wind-up Spider

Use an **axle** and thread to wind the hairy spider up the drain pipe.

You will need:

- strong thread
- a piece of wooden dowel
- masking tape
- an empty cereal box
- a toy spider or paper
- colored pens or paint

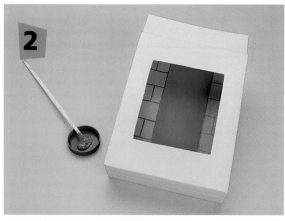

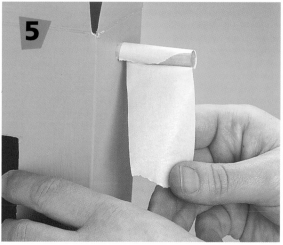

If you do not have a toy spider, draw one on paper, color it, and cut it out.

1 Cut out a large window in the front of the box.

2 Draw or paint a picture of a drain pipe on the inside of the box.

3 Ask an adult to make a hole through each side of the top of the box large enough to push the dowel through.

4 Measure a piece of thread as long as the length of the box. Tie one end to the spider. Tape the other end of the thread to the dowel. Push the dowel through the holes in the box.

5 Wind masking tape around the other end of the dowel to keep it from slipping out.

6 Wind the handle and watch the spider climb the drain pipe.

Glossary

axle rod or bar fixed to the hub of a wheel

cam wheel non-circular wheel

carpenter someone who works with wood

conveyor belt wide, flat loop that turns around to carry something from one end to the other

crank handle joined to the hub of a wheel or axle that is used to turn the wheel or axle

cyclist person riding a bicycle

effort energy used to do something

engine device that uses energy, such as gasoline, to produce power

force push, pull, or twist that makes something move

friction rubbing or "sticking" between two surfaces which happens when one surface moves across the other surface

hub center of the wheel, about which the wheel turns

hydroelectric power station place where electricity is produced from the energy of moving water

pedal lever which is moved with the foot

pyramid three-dimensional shape with a square base and triangular sides. The Ancient Egyptians built huge pyramids of stone.

rim outer edge

roller cylinder that rolls

shaft rod

spokes thin struts that join the rim of a wheel to the hub

tread deep grooves cut into the surface of a tire

turbine machine which produces power, often in the form of electricity

Answers to Questions

p. 11 The smoothest floor should give the least friction.

p. 13 Racing bikes have thin, smooth tires to make them go fast. The wheels are large so that each turn of the pedals makes the bike travel a long way. Mountain bikes have thick tires to help them grip rough ground. The wheels are small so the pedals are easier to turn.

p. 17 All the objects use crank handles. The sewing machine handle turns a wheel. The handle of the car window turns a rod. The handle on the fishing rod turns a roller which winds in the line.

p. 21 The blades of the fan should have a large, slightly curved surface to catch the air.

p. 23 Modern windmills need less wind to make them turn because they are light and are shaped to catch more of the wind.

p. 25 When there was less water in the river, the wheel turned more slowly and so the machines worked more slowly.

p. 27 The water should spurt most forcefully from the bottle with the hole at the bottom.

Index

More Books to Read

Dahl, Michael. *Wheels and Axles.* Danbury, Conn.: Children's Press, 1996.

Grimshaw, Catherine. *Machines.* Chicago: World Book Inc., 1998.

Whittle, Fran. *Simple Machines.* Austin, Tex.: Raintree Steck-Vaughn Publishers, 1997.